THE WEALTH SYSTEM

7 CODES TO MASTER YOUR MONEY, ELIMINATE DEBT, AND BUILD PASSIVE INCOME

INSPIRED LEGACY PRESS

EDGAR HERNÁNDEZ

INSPIRED
LEGACY PRESS

COPYRIGHT

Published by Inspired Legacy Press

Sparks, Nevada, USA

ISBN: 978-1-971513-47-8

Book Design and Layout: Inspired Legacy Press

Logo: Inspired Enterprises LLC

First Edition — 2025

Printed in the United States of America

EPIGRAPH

Money doesn't respond to luck...
it responds to a system.
And once you understand it...
everything changes.
You stop trading your time just to survive...
and start building wealth on your terms.
You break the cycle.
You take back control.
And when you master the Wealth System...
you don't just make money...
you create freedom.

— Edgar Hernández · Inspired Legacy Press

DEDICATION

This book is for those who are done with just surviving.
For those who know they were meant for more...
but were never given the system to achieve it.
For those ready to break the cycle,
to question everything,
and to build a life where money is no longer a limitation...
but a tool.
If you're reading this...
it's not by chance.
This is where your transformation begins.

— Edgar Hernández · Inspired Legacy Press

ACKNOWLEDGMENTS

I'm grateful for every experience that forced me to grow when I had no other choice.

For every mistake that taught me more than any theory ever could.

For every fall that reminded me that progress isn't comfortable... but it's necessary.

To everyone who, consciously or unconsciously, became part of this journey...

because every obstacle, every doubt, and every challenge...

became a key piece in building this system.

I'm also grateful for those who are ready to change their lives...

because this book wouldn't exist without the real demand for transformation.

And above all...

I'm grateful for discipline, vision, and determination...

because without them, no idea ever becomes reality.

This is not just a book.

It's the result of evolution, focus...

and the decision to never settle.

— Edgar Hernández · Inspired Legacy Press

CONTENTS

PROLOGUE

For years, millions of people have followed the same path...

Work hard.

Save what you can.

Hope that one day... things will change.

But the truth is different.

Hard work alone doesn't create wealth.

Discipline without direction doesn't create freedom.

And time... when it's only traded for money... is always lost.

Most people don't have a capacity problem.

They have a system problem.

No one ever taught you how money really works.

No one explained that there are invisible rules...

that determine who moves forward... and who stays stuck.

And until you understand those rules...

you'll keep repeating the same cycle.

This book is not theory.

It's not empty motivation.

And it's definitely not another set of ideas you'll forget in a few days.

This is a system.

A system designed to take you from financial chaos...

to total control.

From debt...

to stability.

From constant effort...

to building automated income.

This isn't about learning how to "make more money"...

it's about learning how to master it.

And when that happens...

your life stops depending on what you do every day...

and starts being built on what you've already created.

If you're reading this...

it's not by accident.

This is the moment you stop improvising...

and start operating with a system.

Because the difference between those who survive...

and those who build real wealth...

isn't luck.

It's the system.

INTRODUCTION

Most people operate within an economic system they don't understand.

They work.

They earn.

They spend.

They repeat.

The process is stable, predictable, and functional at a collective level.

But at an individual level, it has a clear limitation:

It's not designed to build wealth.

The problem isn't a lack of income.

It's the absence of a structure that allows you to keep it, direct it, and multiply it.

That distinction changes everything.

Income is a flow.

Wealth is accumulation.

The first depends on your activity.

The second depends on your system.

As long as you rely solely on your time to generate

money, your growth will always be limited by one unavoidable constraint: the number of hours available to you.

That limit can't be optimized forever.

It can only be surpassed by changing the model.

But most people don't change the model.

They simply increase their participation within it.

They work more.

They chase higher income.

They push harder.

Yet the outcome remains the same.

Because the problem isn't intensity...

it's design.

This is where the real divide appears.

Between those who stay stuck...

and those who move forward with consistency.

It's not about where you start.

It's about how you operate.

Two people can earn the same income for years.

One builds nothing.

The other builds everything.

The difference isn't circumstantial.

It's systematic.

Repeated decisions, guided by a clear structure, create growth.

Isolated decisions, without structure, create fragmentation.

This book is built on that premise.

It doesn't focus on increasing your income as the primary solution.

It focuses on restructuring how you manage it.

Because without control, there is no accumulation.

Without accumulation, there is no investment.

And without investment, there is no scale.

The Wealth System was designed to solve that problem.

It's built around seven codes.

Each one represents a critical level in the process of building wealth:

Mindset.

Control.

Liberation.

Accumulation.

Investment.

Automation.

Scale.

They are not separate concepts.

They are interconnected stages.

The order is not optional.

It's functional.

Trying to invest without control leads to loss.

Trying to scale without structure leads to collapse.

Most people fail not because they lack information...

but because they lack sequence.

This system provides that sequence.

It shows you what to do,

when to do it,

and why it works.

It doesn't promise instant results.

It doesn't remove the need for execution.

But it introduces something most people never have:

A clear operating framework.

When the model is right,

results stop depending on guesswork...

and start responding to structure.

That is the purpose of this book.

Not to motivate.

Not to simplify.

Not to entertain.

But to establish a system that takes you from income to accumulation...

from accumulation to investment...

and from investment to scale.

The process isn't complicated.

But it requires precision.

And it all begins with a single decision:

To stop operating without structure.

PART I

AWAKENING

Throughout history, most people have lived within the same invisible structure:

Trading time for money.

It's not a coincidence.

It's a model.

A model that works well enough to sustain the system...

but not well enough to create freedom.

Since the Industrial Revolution, the value of the individual has been defined by their ability to produce—within a schedule, in a specific place, under conditions set by others. In return, they receive an income.

That model solved a massive economic problem.

But it also created a structural limitation:

Your income is directly tied to your time.

And that leads to an unavoidable consequence:

If your time is finite...

your growth is limited.

This is where the first psychological distortion appears.

Most people don't question the model.

They internalize it.

They believe that if they're not advancing, it's because they're not working hard enough.

Because they lack discipline.

Because something is missing.

But in many cases...

it's not an effort problem.

It's a design problem.

You're operating within a system that isn't built to create wealth...

it's built to sustain a constant flow of labor.

And until you see that...

you'll keep trying to fix the problem from the wrong place.

Work more hours.

Get another job.

Increase your income.

All without realizing that you're increasing intensity...

but not changing the structure.

Personal finance operates on simple principles—

but they are rarely taught:

Active income is linear.

Wealth is exponential.

The first depends on your presence.

The second depends on what you build.

Yet most people never make the transition between the two.

Not because they can't...

but because they were never trained to.

From a psychological standpoint, this creates a repeating pattern:

Earn → Spend → Reset.

No accumulation.

No system.

No direction.

Just constant motion.

And constant motion...

can create the illusion of progress.

But it's not the same as moving forward.

Now consider this:

Two people can earn the same income.

One stays stuck for years.

The other builds stability, then growth... and eventually freedom.

The difference isn't how much they make.

It's how they operate.

The decisions they make.

The structure they follow.

The level of awareness they have about money.

That is the turning point.

The moment you stop reacting...

and start designing.

But that shift doesn't happen automatically.

It requires something specific:

To see what you couldn't see before.

To understand why effort alone wasn't enough.

Why income didn't solve the problem.

And why the model you were following... had a built-in limit.

That is awakening.

It's not motivation.

It's not hype.

It's not temporary energy.

It's clarity.

And once you have clarity...

you can't go back to operating the same way.

This first section is not about giving you quick answers.

It's about something more important:

Restructuring how you understand money, work, and the process of building wealth.

Because if you don't change that first...

everything else will be temporary.

What you're about to read is not a collection of tips.

It's the beginning of a structural shift in how you think.

And that shift...

is the only real starting point.

1

THE ORIGIN OF FINANCIAL STAGNATION

Financial stagnation is rarely the result of a lack of effort.

In most cases, it's the result of operating within a model that was limited from the start.

That model is familiar:

Trading time for money.

It works.

But it has a defining characteristic that is rarely questioned:

It's linear.

Your income is directly tied to how much time you can invest...

and to the value others assign to that time.

That creates two unavoidable constraints:

First, your time is finite.

Second, your control over income is not entirely your own.

Even when you increase your effort, improve your skills, or access better opportunities...

your growth still depends on a variable you cannot expand indefinitely:

Your availability.

This is where the first contradiction appears.

You're told that working more is the solution.

But working more within a linear system...

only increases intensity—it doesn't change the structure.

You may increase your income.

But not necessarily your accumulation.

And without accumulation...

there is no transition to wealth.

This is the critical point.

Because many people confuse temporary improvement with real progress.

Making more money for a period of time doesn't mean the structural problem has been solved.

If money isn't retained, organized, and directed...

the outcome is predictable:

The cycle repeats.

Earn.

Spend.

Reset.

From a practical perspective, this isn't a personal failure.

It's the natural consequence of operating without a system.

Without a defined structure, every financial decision becomes isolated.

No continuity.

No direction.

No sustained accumulation.

Just motion.

And motion, by itself, does not guarantee progress.

Two people can stay in constant motion for years.

One stays in the same place.

The other moves forward consistently.

The difference isn't how much they do.

It's how what they do is structured.

This is where leverage comes into play.

Time-based income is direct:

You work.

You produce.

You get paid.

System-based growth is indirect:

You build.

You structure.

And then you operate on what already exists.

That difference changes everything.

Because in the first case, every result depends on your presence.

In the second, results begin to detach from it.

The problem is that most people never make that transition.

Not because they lack the ability...

but because they keep optimizing a model that has a built-in limit.

They become more efficient within the same structure...

without realizing that the structure itself is the problem.

This creates the illusion of progress.

More income.

More activity.

More effort.

But the end result doesn't change in any meaningful way.

Time remains the dominant factor.

And as long as time is the dominant factor...

your growth will always be limited.

This is where stagnation becomes persistent.

It's not immediate.

It's not obvious at first.

But over time, it becomes undeniable:

No matter how much you try...

there's a ceiling.

That ceiling isn't personal.

It's structural.

And it won't be broken with more effort.

It will be broken with a change in the model.

That change begins when you stop measuring progress solely in terms of income...

and start measuring it in terms of control, accumulation, and the ability to multiply.

That is the first step out of stagnation.

Not doing more...

but operating differently.

Because as long as the model doesn't change...

neither will the result.

2

THE REAL CAUSE OF FINANCIAL DISPERSION

The problem isn't how much money you make.

It's how you manage it.

This idea is often underestimated, because the most common assumption is simple:

More income should lead to a better financial situation.

In reality, it doesn't work that way.

People with very different incomes can end up in the same place.

And people with similar incomes can produce completely different outcomes.

The difference isn't in what comes in.

It's in what happens after.

This is where the most common mistake appears:

Treating money as a flow... but not as a system.

Income comes in.

It gets distributed without structure.

It gets spent without direction.

And the cycle repeats.

No meaningful accumulation.

No defined criteria.

No continuity.

Every financial decision is made in isolation.

That's the problem.

Because without a clear structure, money doesn't organize itself.

It disperses.

From a practical standpoint, this creates a predictable pattern:

Income increases...

and spending adjusts.

Your lifestyle changes...

but your financial position stays the same.

This isn't accidental.

It's structural.

When there's no system of control, money adapts to behavior—not to intention.

And behavior, in the absence of rules, follows immediate impulses:

Comfort.

Consumption.

Reward.

The result is predictable:

No sustained accumulation.

And without accumulation, there is no foundation to build something greater.

This is where most people get stuck.

Because they misdiagnose the problem.

They assume they need to earn more.

But if the pattern doesn't change...

the outcome won't either.

More income, within the same structure...

only amplifies the same behavior.

More spending.

More dispersion.

Same result.

That's why you often see something that doesn't seem to make sense:

People who significantly increase their income...

but never improve their financial position in a meaningful way.

The problem isn't income.

It's the absence of control.

And control is not restriction.

It's direction.

It means deciding—clearly—what role every dollar plays.

What is kept.

What is used.

What is allocated for growth.

Without that level of clarity, money loses its purpose.

It becomes something that comes and goes...

without creating any lasting effect.

That is the critical point.

Because wealth is not built from income...

it's built from what you keep and how you organize it.

This is the first real shift in perspective:

Stop focusing on earning more...

and start focusing on retaining and directing better.

Not as a temporary strategy...

but as a permanent structure.

Because before you can multiply money...

you must learn to control it.

And without control, any attempt at growth will be unstable.

This is the mistake that sustains the cycle.

And it's also the first place where it can be broken.

Not by increasing income...

but by changing how you operate.

PART II

THE WEALTH SYSTEM

Up to this point, you've seen the problem from a structural perspective.

It's not about a lack of effort.

It's not about a lack of income.

It's about operating within a model that doesn't allow sustained accumulation.

Understanding this is necessary.

But it's not enough.

Because identifying the problem doesn't solve it.

It only makes it visible.

What comes next is more demanding:

Replacing the model.

The Wealth System is not a general idea or a collection of isolated recommendations.

It's a sequence.

A process divided into seven levels—each one serving a specific function in the creation of wealth.

The order is not arbitrary.

Ignoring it creates inconsistency.

Following it creates continuity.

Each code answers a specific question:

How you think.

How you control.

How you break free.

How you accumulate.

How you invest.

How you automate.

How you scale.

These stages are not independent.

They function as a system.

The absence of one weakens the others.

The correct execution of one strengthens the next.

This is where most people fail.

Not because they lack information...

but because they lack structure.

They try to invest without control.

They chase additional income without resolving debt.

They increase capacity without defining a system.

The result is instability.

Because without sequence, there is no consistency.

This model corrects that problem.

It doesn't simplify the process.

It organizes it.

It defines what to build first.

What to optimize next.

And when to scale.

It doesn't depend on extraordinary conditions.

But it does require something specific:

Intentional execution.

Each code demands an adjustment in how you operate.

Not just in what you do...

but in how you decide.

That shift is progressive.

It doesn't happen instantly.

But when executed correctly, it compounds.

And over time, that accumulation becomes undeniable.

That is the purpose of this section.

Not to present ideas.

But to establish an operating system.

Because when the structure is clear...

execution stops being confusing.

And when execution is consistent...

results stop being random.

From this point forward, the focus shifts:

From understanding...

to execution.

And that shift defines everything that follows.

3

CODE 1 — THE WEALTH MINDSET

Before you can change any financial result, you must change the point from which your decisions are made.

That point isn't visible.

It's not your income.

It's not your spending.

It's not your investments.

It's your interpretation.

The way you understand money directly determines how you use it.

Two individuals can face the exact same financial situation and act in completely different ways—not because of differences in ability, but because of differences in judgment.

That judgment doesn't appear on its own.

It is formed over time—through references, experiences, and observed models.

The problem is that, in most cases, this process happens without intention.

Ideas are adopted without analysis.

Patterns are repeated without questioning.

Decisions are made without understanding their origin.

And over time, that becomes a way of operating.

This is where the first structural limitation appears.

It's not a lack of information.

It's the misinterpretation of the information available.

Money is not managed through technical knowledge alone.

It's managed through judgment.

What you consider a good decision.

What you perceive as risk.

What you prioritize in the short term versus the long term.

Without a clear framework, these variables are resolved inconsistently.

And inconsistency, sustained over time, prevents any real process of accumulation.

That's why, before discussing control, investment, or growth...

you must establish a different foundation.

Not in what you do...

but in how you decide.

Mindset, in this context, is not an abstract idea or a positive attitude.

It's an operating structure.

It defines how you interpret value.

How you evaluate opportunities.

And how you allocate resources.

Without that structure, any system becomes unstable.

Because the decisions that support it lack coherence.

This code is not about changing what you think at a superficial level.

It aims for something more precise:

To reorganize the framework from which you operate.

That means identifying your current model, understanding its limitations, and replacing it with one that works.

It's not immediate.

But it is necessary.

Because every code that follows depends on this one.

Control requires judgment.

Investment requires understanding.

Scale requires direction.

And none of those can be sustained without a clear mental foundation.

This is the true starting point of the system.

Not a technique.

Not a tool.

But a different way of understanding the game.

And that difference—though invisible at first—

ends up defining everything else.

4

CHAPTER 1 — THE WRONG MENTAL MODEL

Most financial decisions are not the result of conscious analysis.

They are the result of patterns.

Patterns acquired over time, repeated without questioning, and executed automatically.

That collection of patterns forms what can be defined as a mental model—

a framework through which you interpret money, work, and value.

The problem isn't having a model.

The problem is not knowing which one you're operating from.

Because when it's not identified, it can't be evaluated.

And when it's not evaluated...

it's assumed to be correct.

In most cases, that model has a common origin:

Trading time for stability.

Security is prioritized.

Uncertainty is avoided.

Predictability is valued over growth.

This approach is understandable.

It allows you to maintain income, reduce immediate risk, and sustain a functional structure.

But it has a clear limitation:

It's not designed to build wealth.

It's designed to maintain continuity.

Under this model, decisions follow a specific logic:

Immediate income is prioritized.

Any variation that could threaten it is avoided.

The short term is valued over the long term.

This has consequences.

First, it limits your ability to take calculated risks.

Not because risk is inherently negative...

but because it isn't properly understood.

Second, it prevents the transition toward structures that don't depend directly on your time.

You remain within what is familiar—even when that model has an obvious limit.

Third, it creates a false sense of progress.

You work more.

You earn more.

But you don't build.

The outcome is consistent with the model:

There is movement...

but no meaningful accumulation.

This is where the contradiction appears.

You try to improve results without changing the framework that produces them.

You attempt to optimize within the same system that creates the limitation.

And by definition...

that has a limited ceiling.

This mental model has three defining characteristics:

It is automatic. Decisions are not questioned—they are executed.

It is reactive. You respond to circumstances instead of anticipating them.

It is linear. Growth is assumed to come only from increased effort.

As long as these conditions remain...

the result is predictable:

Stability without expansion.

The problem is not that this model is entirely wrong.

The problem is using it as your only way of operating.

Because when no alternative exists...

there is no possibility of transition.

And without transition...

there is no structural change.

This is where the adjustment begins.

Not by adding more information...

but by identifying the model you're currently operating within.

Understanding how you decide.

What you prioritize.

And the logic behind your actions.

Because without that clarity...

any attempt at improvement will be superficial.

This chapter is not about immediately replacing the model.

It's about making it visible.

Because only when it becomes visible...

can it be changed.

And that is the first real step within the system.

Not changing what you do...
but understanding where you're operating from.

5

CHAPTER 2 — THINKING IN SYSTEMS, NOT INCOME

The most important shift in how you operate doesn't happen when you earn more money.

It happens when you stop thinking in terms of income...

and start thinking in terms of systems.

That distinction changes everything.

Income is the result.

The system is what produces it.

Yet most people focus only on the result.

They look for better opportunities.

Higher salaries.

Better conditions.

But they never change the structure that produces those results.

And without a structural shift...

any improvement is temporary.

Because income, on its own, is unstable.

It depends on external conditions—
demand, available time, and constant participation.
A system, on the other hand, organizes those variables.
It defines how income is generated,
how it is distributed,
and how it is transformed into accumulation.

That difference completely changes how decisions are made.

When you think in terms of income, your decisions are immediate.

You evaluate how much you can earn.
Which option pays more.
Which path delivers the fastest return.

When you think in terms of systems, your decisions are structural.

You evaluate sustainability.
Repeatability.
And long-term growth potential.
You don't focus only on what comes in...
you focus on what stays—and how it evolves.
This shift is not intuitive.

It requires letting go of immediate results as your primary metric.

Because the immediate, while necessary...
does not build on its own.
It can generate cash flow—
but not necessarily progress.
Here's where another key distinction appears:
Income responds to activity.
A system responds to design.
If activity stops, income declines.
But if the system is properly built...

results can remain—or even grow.

This is where the transition begins.

Not when you earn more...

but when you stop depending exclusively on direct activity.

And for that to happen, your focus must change:

From constant execution...

to deliberate construction.

This means understanding that every financial decision is not isolated.

It is part of a larger structure.

A purchase is not just an expense—

it's an allocation within a system.

Income is not just money coming in—

it's a variable within a larger framework.

And when those variables are not organized...

the outcome becomes inconsistent.

That's why thinking in systems requires rules.

What percentage is retained.

What is allocated for growth.

What is used.

Not as general advice—

but as a defined structure.

Without that structure, money has no direction.

And without direction...

there is no sustained accumulation.

This is where the logic changes.

It's no longer about maximizing each individual income.

It's about optimizing the whole system.

Because wealth is not built through isolated decisions—

it's built through the consistency of a structure.

That is the core principle of this chapter.

Stop focusing only on how much money comes in...

and start defining how the system that manages it actually works.

Because when the system is right...

income stops being the main problem.

And once it's no longer the problem...

it becomes a tool.

6

CHAPTER 3 — OPERATING WITH INTENTION

Once the mental model has been identified and the logic of the system is understood, there's one step that is often overlooked:

How you execute.

Understanding is not enough.

Many people grasp sound financial concepts...

yet continue to operate the same way.

Not because they lack ability—

but because they lack intention in their decisions.

This is where the gap between knowledge and application becomes clear.

Knowledge explains.

Intention directs.

Without intention, decisions default back to automatic behavior.

You spend without evaluating.

You earn without planning.

You decide without structure.

And the outcome inevitably reflects that pattern.

Operating with intention means interrupting that automatic process.

Not reacting—

but deciding.

Every financial move stops being circumstantial...

and becomes deliberate.

This doesn't mean overcomplicating every action.

It means assigning it a clear purpose.

Why you spend.

Why you retain.

Why you allocate resources in a specific way.

Without that clarity, money loses its function.

It becomes a resource without direction—

flowing in and out without creating accumulation.

Intention introduces order.

It defines priorities.

It establishes boundaries.

And it creates alignment between what you want... and what you do.

This point is critical, because it connects directly to the next level of the system.

You cannot control what you don't clearly observe.

And you cannot clearly observe...

what you don't consciously decide.

That's why operating with intention is not a suggestion.

It's a requirement.

Every decision becomes part of a structure.

Every action contributes to a cumulative result.

And over time, that consistency creates separation.

Not immediately.

Not visibly at first.

But inevitably.

Because when the way you operate changes...
your results stop being accidental.
And that shift doesn't come from more information.
It happens when every decision stops being automatic...
and becomes intentional.

7

CODE 2 — TOTAL MONEY CONTROL

Most people don't lose money because they don't earn enough.

They lose it because they lack control.

This idea isn't intuitive—

but it is accurate.

Without a system of control, any level of income—no matter how large—

will eventually disperse.

Not by chance.

By design.

Money, without direction, follows the path of least resistance.

It adapts to behavior.

It responds to habits.

And it ends up where it was never intended to go.

This is where the second structural problem appears.

People try to grow without first establishing control.

They attempt to invest without knowing how much they can actually retain.

They try to scale without building a stable foundation.

And the result is instability.

Because growth without control cannot be sustained.

Control is not restriction.

It's not about limiting how money is used—

it's about defining its function.

Every dollar must have a purpose.

What is retained.

What is used.

What is allocated for growth.

Without that definition, money loses coherence.

It becomes flow without structure.

And flow without structure...

does not create accumulation.

This is where most people get stuck.

Not because they don't earn enough—

but because they don't know what they actually have available.

They confuse income with capacity.

But not everything that comes in...

can be used.

One part must sustain the present.

Another must build the future.

And that division cannot be arbitrary.

It must be defined.

Control introduces that definition.

It creates clarity.

How much comes in.

How much is retained.

And where it is directed.

Without that visibility, there are no informed decisions.

And without informed decisions...
there is no consistent progress.
This is where real accumulation begins.
Not by increasing income—
but by systematically retaining a portion of it.
Because before you can multiply money...
you must stop its dispersion.
This code establishes that foundation.
Not as an isolated technique—
but as a permanent structure.
Because once money is controlled...
it stops being unpredictable.
And once it stops being unpredictable...
it can be directed.
That is the starting point for everything that follows.

8

CHAPTER 4 — THE LACK OF FINANCIAL VISIBILITY

You can't control what you can't see.

This is one of the most common limitations in money management—

and at the same time, one of the least recognized.

Most people don't have an income problem.

They have a visibility problem.

They know how much they earn.

But they don't know how much they actually keep.

Or how what they spend is truly distributed.

That distinction is critical.

Income is a general figure.

Distribution is a structure.

And without understanding that structure...

any attempt at control is incomplete.

This is where the problem begins.

Money comes in...

but it isn't tracked.

It's used without clear records.

It's allocated without defined criteria.

And at the end of the period, the outcome is unclear.

There's no precise understanding of where it went...

or how much could have been retained.

This isn't an isolated mistake.

It's a way of operating.

A way where money is treated as a continuous flow...

but not as a system that requires tracking.

From a practical standpoint, this makes improvement impossible.

Because without clear data...

there is nothing to adjust.

You can't optimize what you don't understand.

And you can't understand what you don't observe.

This is where visibility becomes essential.

Not as a complex tool—

but as a foundational principle:

Knowing exactly what is happening with every dollar.

How much comes in.

How much is retained.

And where it is directed.

Without that clarity, money loses traceability.

And once it loses traceability...

it loses control.

This point is often underestimated because it doesn't create immediate change.

Tracking, observing, and organizing don't produce visible results in the short term.

But they establish something far more important:

Decision-making power.

Because once the information is clear...

decisions stop being intuitive...

and become intentional.

This is the first step within total control.
Not adjusting behavior immediately—
but understanding it.
Not changing results right away—
but making them visible.
Because only when money stops being vague...
can it begin to be directed.
And without direction...
there is no structure.
And without structure...
there is no growth.

9

CHAPTER 5 — DEFINING CONTROL: STRUCTURE AND RULES

Visibility allows you to understand the problem.

Control allows you to correct it.

But control does not happen on its own.

It is not an automatic result of observing your money.

It is a structural decision.

It requires defining rules.

Because without rules...

behavior defaults back to automatic.

You spend based on the moment.

You decide based on urgency.

And money continues to move without direction.

This is where an important distinction appears:

Control is not restriction.

It's not about limiting how money is used—

it's about organizing it under a clear framework.

Every dollar must serve a function.

Not as a general idea...

but as a defined structure.

What portion sustains the present.
What portion is retained.
What portion is allocated for growth.
Without that definition, money loses coherence.
It adapts to circumstances...
but it does not respond to a goal.
This is where most people fail.
Because they try to control without establishing rules.
They observe their money...
but they don't organize it.
And without organization...
information does not create change.
This is where control becomes a system.
It's not enough to know how much you have.
You must decide how it is distributed.
That distribution cannot depend on emotions...
or on temporary circumstances.
It must follow a logic.
A logic that remains consistent over time.
Because consistency is what creates accumulation.
Without consistency...
every cycle resets.
Each income is handled differently.
Each decision is made without reference.
And the result is instability.
Control introduces stability.
It reduces variability.
It defines boundaries.
And it allows money to fulfill a specific function.
This process does not require complexity.
It requires clarity.
Set percentages.
Define priorities.

Assign purpose.

And above all...

follow the structure.

Because a rule that is not applied...

is not a rule.

It's an intention.

And intentions do not produce results.

Structures do.

This is the point where money stops being reactive...

and starts being directed.

Not because the amount changes—

but because the way it is organized changes.

And when organization is correct...

accumulation stops being occasional...

and becomes progressive.

That is the purpose of this chapter.

Not to observe.

Not to analyze.

But to define.

Because once control is established...

money stops being uncertain.

And once it stops being uncertain...

it can begin to grow.

10

CHAPTER 6 — APPLYING CONTROL IN PRACTICE

Control is not defined in theory.

It is proven through execution.

Up to this point, the structure has been clear:

Visibility to understand.

Rules to organize.

But neither of these produces results on its own.

The shift happens when both are applied consistently.

This is where most people fail.

Not because they don't understand what to do—

but because they don't integrate it into how they operate.

Control stops being effective when it is applied inconsistently.

Tracking for a few days.

Organizing only under pressure.

Adjusting only when money runs low.

That approach doesn't create stability.

It creates reaction.

And reacting is not the same as controlling.

Control requires continuity.

Every income is tracked.

Every decision is evaluated.

Every allocation follows the same structure.

Without exception.

Because a repeated exception...

stops being an exception—and becomes a pattern.

This is the critical point.

The system doesn't fail because of poor design.

It fails because of a lack of consistency.

And consistency is not intensity.

It doesn't require extreme effort—

it requires precise repetition.

Applying control in practice means operating under the same rules—

regardless of the amount.

When income is high.

When income is low.

When there is pressure.

And when there isn't.

Because the goal is not to react to money—

but to direct it.

This requires something specific:

Eliminating improvisation.

Every dollar already has a defined destination.

Every use already has an assigned function.

Decisions are not made in the moment—

they are executed based on what was already defined.

That is the difference between intention and system.

Intention decides in the present.

The system decides in advance.

This approach reduces friction.

It removes unnecessary decisions.

And eliminates dependence on emotional states.

Money stops depending on how you feel...

and starts depending on how you operate.

That shift is fundamental.

Because most people don't lose control due to lack of knowledge—

but due to inconsistency in execution.

Applying control is not complex.

But it is demanding.

It requires maintaining the structure—

even when it doesn't seem necessary.

Because those are the moments where the difference is defined.

The result of this process is not immediate.

But it is cumulative.

And accumulation, sustained over time...

creates stability.

That stability is the foundation.

Without it, you cannot move to the next level.

With it...

everything else becomes possible.

Because when money is under control...

it stops being unpredictable.

And once it stops being unpredictable...

it can be used with precision.

11

CODE 3 — DEBT LIBERATION

Debt is not just a financial obligation.

It is an operational limitation.

It reduces your ability to decide.

It commits your future income.

And it conditions every attempt at growth.

From a structural perspective, debt acts as a drag.

It doesn't stop progress entirely...

but it slows it down and increases friction.

That's why trying to build wealth without properly managing debt creates instability.

You try to invest without freeing up cash flow.

You try to accumulate while capital is constantly leaking out.

And the result is inconsistency.

Because the system is divided.

One part is trying to grow.

The other is tied to past decisions.

This is where the distinction appears:

Functional debt vs. limiting debt.
Not all debt is inherently bad.
But all poorly managed debt is.
When there is no clear strategy to eliminate it...
it becomes a cycle.
Minimum payments.
Accumulating interest.
Reset.
That cycle doesn't break through intention.
It breaks through structure.
Most people make a specific mistake:
They try to eliminate debt without a system.
They pay what they can.
They prioritize what feels urgent.
They react to pressure.
But they don't follow a defined strategy.
And without a strategy...
there is no measurable progress.
Debt liberation is not just about how much you pay.
It's about how the process is structured.
Which debt you attack first.
Under what logic.
And with what level of consistency.
Without that structure, progress is slow—
and often reversible.
Because until the root of the problem is addressed...
the cycle can repeat.
This code is not about eliminating all debt immediately.
It's about building a system to exit debt permanently.
To regain control over your cash flow.
To reduce friction.
And to restore operational capacity.

Because only when your flow is no longer compromised...

can the system move to the next level.

That is the objective.

Not to react to debt...

but to resolve it structurally.

And that process begins with a clear decision:

To stop sustaining the cycle.

12

CHAPTER 7 — THE TRUE NATURE OF DEBT

Most people understand debt as an obligation.

Something that must be paid.

Something that must be resolved.

Something that, over time, will disappear.

But that is an incomplete interpretation.

Debt is not just an amount owed.

It is a transfer of control.

Every time you carry debt, a portion of your future income...

no longer fully belongs to you.

It is already committed.

And that changes how it should be understood.

Because it's not just about how much you owe—

it's about how much of your future capacity has already been assigned.

And that assignment has consequences.

It reduces your margin of decision.

It limits your ability to invest.

And it constrains your growth.

From a structural perspective, debt introduces rigidity.

It forces you to maintain constant cash flow.

It prevents you from reducing activity.

And it increases your exposure to risk in the face of disruption.

That's why debt is not neutral.

It directly affects your system.

This is where an important distinction appears—one that is rarely explained with clarity:

Not all debt is the same...

but all debt carries a cost beyond interest.

That cost is operational.

Less flexibility.

Less room to maneuver.

Less capacity to build.

Most people evaluate debt in purely financial terms:

Interest rate.

Term.

Balance.

But they rarely evaluate it in structural terms:

How it affects their cash flow.

How it limits their decisions.

How it shapes their future.

And that's where the mistake happens.

Because a debt may look manageable on paper...

but restrictive in structure.

This is where the problem becomes persistent.

It gets normalized.

It's accepted as part of the system.

As something inevitable.

As a standard condition.

And once it's normalized...

it stops being questioned.

But debt is not meant to be permanent.

It is meant to be transitional.

A tool, in certain contexts—

but never a foundation.

The problem is that without a clear strategy, it stops being a tool...

and becomes a cycle.

Minimum payments.

Interest accumulation.

Continuation.

That pattern doesn't break through intention.

It breaks when your understanding changes.

When debt stops being seen as "normal"...

and is recognized as a direct limitation on your system.

That is the first real shift.

Not paying more.

Not paying faster.

But understanding exactly what debt represents.

Because once you understand that every debt reduces your ability to build...

your priorities change.

It stops being just another obligation...

and becomes a critical constraint.

And only when that constraint is clearly recognized...

can it begin to be resolved—permanently.

13

CHAPTER 8 — STRUCTURING DEBT ELIMINATION

Getting out of debt is not an act of effort.

It's a process of organization.

Most people try to solve it by increasing payments in a disorganized way.

They pay what they can.

They prioritize what feels urgent.

They react to immediate pressure.

But that approach does not produce consistent results.

It produces partial progress...

and in many cases, reversible outcomes.

Because the problem isn't how much you pay.

It's how the process is structured.

Without a clear structure, the money allocated to debt competes with everything else:

Daily expenses.

Consumption.

Impulsive decisions.

And in that competition...

debt rarely wins.

That's why the first step is not to pay more.

It's to define a strategy.

A strategy requires order.

Which debt is addressed first.

Under what criteria.

And with what level of consistency.

There are multiple approaches, but they all share one principle:

Debt elimination requires concentrated focus—not dispersion.

Dividing efforts across multiple obligations at the same time reduces impact.

Concentrating resources on one, on the other hand, accelerates the process.

This is not intuitive for most people.

Distributing payments feels safer.

But that distribution dilutes progress.

Real progress happens when there is a clear priority.

One debt becomes the primary target.

The others remain stable.

And once the first is eliminated...

the freed resources are redirected to the next.

This process creates something critical:

Compounding progression.

Each debt eliminated doesn't just reduce the burden—

it increases your capacity.

More available cash flow.

Greater speed.

Less friction.

That is the effect most people overlook.

Getting out of debt is not just about reducing a number.

It's about restoring operational capacity.

This is where consistency becomes decisive.
It's not about making a one-time effort—
it's about maintaining continuous execution.
Every cycle.
Every income.
Under the same logic.
Without unnecessary interruptions.
Because every interruption delays the process...
and extends the limitation.
This is where the focus shifts.
Debt stops being something you handle occasionally...
and becomes a structural priority.
Not because it's urgent—
but because it's limiting.
And anything that limits the system...
must be resolved before you attempt to scale.
This chapter is not about extreme speed.
It's about correct direction.
Because when the structure is right...
progress stops depending on extra effort
and starts responding to organization.
That is the principle.
Not paying more out of impulse...
but eliminating with strategy.
And when that strategy is applied consistently...
debt stops being permanent
and becomes a process with a defined end.

14

CHAPTER 9 — REGAINING CONTROL OF CASH FLOW

Eliminating debt is not the final goal.

It's the point of release.

Because once debt is reduced or eliminated, something happens that most people don't anticipate:

Your cash flow changes.

Money that was previously committed stops leaving.

Obligations decrease.

And available capacity increases.

But this moment—one that should represent progress—is often wasted.

Because without a clear structure...

the freed money is not retained.

It is redistributed automatically.

More consumption.

More spending.

Same result.

Debt disappears...

but the system remains the same.

And when the system doesn't change...

the problem repeats itself.

This is where one of the most critical mistakes occurs:

Confusing relief with progress.

Reducing debt creates relief.

But only changing the structure creates progress.

If the freed cash flow is not redirected...

it does not become accumulation.

And without accumulation...

there is no transition to growth.

That's why this moment is critical.

Because it determines whether liberation becomes progress...

or just another repetition of the cycle.

Regaining control of your cash flow requires something specific:

Deciding what happens to your money before it arrives.

Not waiting until you have it to decide.

Not reacting in the moment.

But assigning it a function in advance.

The money that was previously used for debt does not disappear.

It changes purpose.

It can become accumulation.

Future investment.

Structural growth.

But only if it is directed.

Otherwise, it dissipates.

This is where control becomes consolidated.

Not only do you stop losing money—

you begin to build.

Because cash flow, when it is free and properly directed...

becomes the foundation of growth.

This is where an important transition occurs:

From paying...

to retaining.

From retaining...

to accumulating.

And that accumulation, over time...

allows you to move to the next level of the system.

But that transition is not automatic.

It depends on a clear decision:

Not increasing your level of consumption

at the same pace as your capacity increases.

Because that is the pattern that sustains the cycle:

More income.

More spending.

Same result.

Breaking that pattern requires intention.

It requires defining limits—

and maintaining them.

Because cash flow, without direction...

will always find a way out.

But when it is controlled and assigned with purpose...

it becomes a tool.

And at that point, money stops being an obligation you manage...

and becomes a resource you build.

That is the true conclusion of this code.

Not just eliminating debt—

but regaining control over what comes next.

Because that is where growth begins.

15

CODE 4 — INTELLIGENT ACCUMULATION

Accumulation is not the result of earning more money. **It is the result of consistently retaining a portion of it.**

That distinction changes everything.

Because most people associate financial growth with increasing income...

when in reality, it depends on your ability to keep and organize what you already have.

Without accumulation, there is no starting point.

No base.

No margin.

No capacity to build.

That's why trying to invest or scale without first accumulating...

creates instability.

You attempt to grow without a foundation.

And the result is inconsistent.

Accumulation creates stability.

It allows you to absorb fluctuations.

It reduces dependency.

And it builds a base from which you can operate with precision.

But it does not happen through intention alone.

It happens through a system.

Saving occasionally does not create accumulation.

It requires consistency.

It requires defining a portion of your income that is not consumed.

Not as a one-time decision...

but as a permanent rule.

This is where a critical difference appears.

Most people save what's left over.

A system accumulates first.

That shift completely changes the outcome.

Because anything that depends on what "remains" is variable.

And what is variable does not create structure.

Accumulation, on the other hand, requires priority.

It is defined before spending—

not after.

This principle is simple, but rarely applied.

And its impact is direct.

Because every cycle in which you retain a portion of your income...

you build capacity.

Not visible at first—

but compounding over time.

This is where most people lose continuity.

Not because they can't accumulate—

but because they interrupt the process.

They adjust when there is pressure.

They stop when there is comfort.

And by doing so...

they reset the cycle.

Accumulation does not work in interruptions.

It works through repetition.

Every income.

Every cycle.

Under the same structure.

Without depending on how things feel in the moment.

This code establishes that logic.

Not as a temporary strategy—

but as a permanent foundation of the system.

Because without accumulation...

there is no transition to investment.

And without investment...

there is no exponential growth.

This is the point where money stops being just flow...

and starts becoming capital.

And that difference—though small at the beginning—

ends up defining the entire process.

Because wealth does not begin when you earn more.

It begins when you stop consuming everything you earn.

16

CHAPTER 10 — WHY MOST PEOPLE FAIL TO ACCUMULATE

Accumulation does not fail because of a lack of income.

It fails because of a lack of consistency.

Most people, at some point, have the ability to retain a portion of their money.

The problem is...

they don't do it consistently.

They save when there's surplus.

They stop when there's pressure.

They resume when conditions improve.

And by doing so...

they interrupt the process.

This pattern is common because accumulation is perceived as secondary.

Something you do "when you can."

But that approach is incompatible with the result you want.

Because what depends on conditions...

does not create structure.

And without structure...

there is no real accumulation.

This is where a critical misconception appears.

People assume accumulation requires large amounts.

But accumulation does not depend on the initial size.

It depends on repetition.

Small amounts, sustained over time...

build capacity.

Large amounts, interrupted...

do not.

This is the point most people overlook.

Because they focus on how much they can save...

instead of how long they can sustain it.

And sustainability is what defines the outcome.

Another factor that prevents accumulation is the lack of priority.

Money is allocated first to consumption.

Then to immediate obligations.

And only afterward—if anything remains—to saving.

But what remains is variable.

And what is variable does not build.

Accumulation requires a different order.

It must happen before spending—

not after.

Because when it's left for last...

it competes with everything else.

And in that competition...

it rarely survives.

There is also a psychological component.

The benefit of accumulation is not immediate.

It doesn't create instant reward.

It doesn't produce visible change in the short term.

That's why it feels less important.

Consumption, on the other hand, delivers immediate feedback:

Satisfaction.

Comfort.

Reward.

And human behavior naturally prioritizes the immediate...

over the cumulative.

This pattern is not a personal flaw.

It's a natural tendency.

But when left uncorrected...

it prevents any form of long-term construction.

This is where the system creates a difference.

It does not depend on motivation.

It depends on structure.

It defines a fixed proportion.

It executes it consistently.

And it removes the need to decide each time.

Because constant decision-making...

creates friction.

And friction reduces consistency.

Accumulation does not require repeated decisions.

It requires clear rules.

And once those rules are defined...

the process becomes automatic.

That is the point where results begin to change.

Not when you have more money...

but when you stop depending on the moment to decide.

Because as long as accumulation depends on how you feel...

it will never be stable.

But when it depends on structure...
it becomes inevitable.
That is the principle.
Not saving when you can—
but building a system where saving is part of the process.

17

CHAPTER 11 — STRUCTURING ACCUMULATION THE RIGHT WAY

Accumulation does not happen through intention.

It happens by design.

Once you understand why most people fail to accumulate, the next step is not to try harder—

it's to build a structure that makes it inevitable.

Without structure, accumulation depends on the moment.

With structure, it depends on the system.

This is the turning point.

Effective accumulation begins when you define a fixed percentage of your income that is not consumed.

Not as a general guideline—

but as a permanent rule.

That percentage is not arbitrary.

It must be significant enough to create progress...

yet sustainable enough to maintain over time.

This is where many people fail.

They try to accumulate too much, too quickly.

They create pressure.

And eventually, they abandon the process.

Accumulation does not require intensity.

It requires continuity.

That's why the structure must be realistic.

Applicable at any income level.

Sustainable under different conditions.

Because the goal is not to accumulate once.

It's to accumulate always.

Once the percentage is defined, the next step is order.

Accumulation must happen first.

Not after spending.

Not when something is left over.

Before.

This shift is decisive.

Because it removes competition with consumption.

The money that is accumulated is no longer available for impulsive decisions.

It is separated.

It is protected.

And it begins to serve a different purpose.

This is where money begins to transform into capital.

But the structure doesn't end there.

You must also define the destination of that accumulation.

Not all retained money serves the same function.

One portion should remain as a reserve.

Another can be prepared for future investment.

Without this distinction...

accumulation loses efficiency.

It is preserved—

but not optimized.

The correct structure creates clarity.

It defines categories.

It assigns functions.

And it allows every portion of money to serve a specific purpose.

This reduces uncertainty.

It eliminates unnecessary decisions.

And it reinforces consistency.

Because when the system is defined...

execution becomes simple.

You don't decide in every moment—

you follow what has already been established.

That is the core principle of intelligent accumulation.

It does not depend on how much you earn.

It depends on how you structure what you have.

And when that structure is clear...

accumulation stops being an effort...

and becomes a consequence.

That is the purpose of this chapter.

Not to motivate saving—

but to define how to do it correctly.

Because when accumulation becomes part of the system...

growth stops being uncertain.

18

CHAPTER 12 — SUSTAINING ACCUMULATION OVER TIME

Accumulation is not lost due to lack of ability.

It is lost through interruption.

Most people can accumulate for a period of time.

The problem is they can't sustain it.

The system is applied when there is clarity.

It weakens when conditions change.

And it gets abandoned when it no longer feels necessary.

This pattern is common.

Because when accumulation starts producing results...

it creates a false sense of stability.

It feels "enough."

Pressure decreases.

And gradually, the rules begin to relax.

That is the point where the system starts to fail.

Not immediately—

but progressively.

One cycle is skipped.

A percentage is adjusted.

An exception is allowed.

And each adjustment introduces variability.

Variability breaks consistency.

And without consistency... there is no sustained accumulation.

This is where the difference between intention and structure becomes clear.

Intention depends on context.

Structure remains despite it.

Sustaining accumulation requires something specific:

Eliminating internal negotiation.

Not deciding each time.

Not constantly evaluating whether it's "worth it."

Just executing.

Because every repeated decision introduces friction.

And friction, over time...

reduces adherence to the system.

That's why accumulation should not depend on constant discipline.

It should depend on design.

A design where the percentage is already defined.

Where the order is already established.

And where execution does not require additional analysis.

This is the point where accumulation stops being an action...

and becomes a condition.

It happens with every income.

Every cycle.

Without exception.

Regardless of the environment.

Because the environment always changes.

Income fluctuates.

Needs evolve.

Circumstances shift.

But the structure should not.

Not because it is rigid—

but because it is the foundation that allows everything else to adapt.

This is where most people get it wrong.

They adjust the system based on the moment...

instead of adjusting the moment to fit the system.

And that shift in perspective is decisive.

Because when the system holds...

results compound.

Not visibly at first—

but inevitably over time.

Sustained accumulation creates stability.

Stability creates margin.

And margin allows you to move to the next level.

This is the completion of the process.

Not accumulating more.

Not accumulating faster.

But accumulating without interruption.

Because the difference between those who build...

and those who stay in the same place...

is not what they do once.

It's what they are able to sustain.

And when accumulation becomes part of the system...

it stops depending on conscious effort...

and becomes a permanent advantage.

19

CODE 5 — CONSISTENT INVESTING

Accumulation creates stability.

Investing creates growth.

Without accumulation, there is no starting point.

Without investing, there is no expansion.

This is the next level of the system.

But it is also one of the most misunderstood.

Most people see investing as something complex—

reserved for those with large amounts of money or specialized knowledge.

So they delay it.

They wait for the "right time."

More capital.

More certainty.

And by doing so...

they delay the most important transition in the system:

From static money...

to productive money.

Accumulated money, on its own, does not grow significantly.

It preserves value.

It protects stability.

But it does not create real expansion.

For that to happen, it must enter a productive system.

It must work.

This is where a key distinction appears.

Most people try to invest occasionally.

They look for specific opportunities.

They try to "get it right."

They depend on timing.

But that approach creates a problem:

Inconsistency.

And inconsistency, in investing...

limits any meaningful result.

Investing is not built on isolated decisions.

It is built on repetition.

It does not depend on finding the perfect opportunity.

It depends on consistent participation in a system that produces value.

This shift in perspective is fundamental.

Stop thinking of investing as an event...

and start understanding it as a process.

A process where every contribution becomes part of a larger structure.

Where time works in your favor.

And consistency reduces dependence on timing.

This is where investing connects directly to the system.

It's not about how much you invest once.

It's about how much you invest consistently.

Because exponential growth does not come from a single action.

It comes from accumulation applied over time.

And time only works when there is continuity.

This code is not about making investing complex.

It's about making it operational.

Defining when to start.

How to participate.

And how to sustain the process without interruption.

Because the most common mistake is not investing poorly.

It's not investing at all.

Or doing it inconsistently.

And in both cases, the result is the same:

Money remains static.

This is the point where the system changes its nature.

From preserving...

to multiplying.

And that shift does not come from additional knowledge.

It happens when money stops depending solely on the person who earns it...

and begins to produce on its own.

That is the objective of this code.

Not to maximize short-term results—

but to build a process that, sustained over time, creates real growth.

Because when investing is consistent...

growth stops being linear.

And when it stops being linear...

the difference becomes significant.

20

CHAPTER 13 — WHY MOST PEOPLE DON'T INVEST

Most people don't lose money by investing.

They lose growth by not investing.

This is a critical point that is often misunderstood.

The assumption is that the main risk is doing it wrong.

But in reality, the biggest risk is not participating at all.

Not because investing guarantees immediate results...

but because not investing guarantees stagnation.

This is where the first obstacle appears:

The perception of complexity.

People believe investing requires advanced knowledge, experience, or special conditions.

And that perception delays action.

They wait to understand more.

They wait for the right moment.

They wait for greater certainty.

But that waiting has a cost:

Time.

And in investing, time is not a secondary factor.

It is the primary one.

Every period without participation is a period where capital produces nothing.

It doesn't grow.

It doesn't compound.

It remains static.

And in this context, growth is not lost because of a bad decision...

it is lost because of inaction.

The second obstacle is the search for certainty.

People try to eliminate risk before they begin.

They overanalyze.

They compare endlessly.

They postpone the decision.

But investing does not operate under conditions of absolute certainty.

It operates under probability.

And waiting for certainty in a probabilistic environment...

is a form of inaction.

The third obstacle is inconsistency.

Even when people start...

they don't sustain it.

They invest once.

They stop.

They try again later.

This pattern eliminates the main advantage of the system:

Compounding over time.

Because isolated investing does not create meaningful results.

It is repetition that creates impact.

Without continuity...

the process loses its power.

Another key factor is the perception of amount.

People believe they need large sums to begin.

And when they don't have them...

they delay the decision.

But this approach ignores a fundamental principle:

Investing does not depend on the starting size.

It depends on consistency.

Small amounts, sustained over time...

build structure.

Large amounts, without continuity...

do not.

This misconception keeps many people out of the process.

Not because they lack the ability...

but because they hold the wrong expectation.

This is where the system creates clarity.

Investing is not a one-time event.

It is a function of the model.

It happens within a structure.

On a recurring basis.

Without depending on timing.

You're not trying to get it right.

You're trying to participate.

Because over the long term, consistent participation reduces dependence on individual decisions—

and allows the system to do the work.

This is the turning point.

Not when you understand investing...

but when you stop postponing it.

Because every period that passes without participation...

is not neutral.

It is an opportunity that is not compounding.
And in investing...
compounding is what defines the outcome.
That is the core mistake.
Not investing poorly—
but not investing at all.
And as long as that pattern continues...
growth will remain limited.
Not because of a lack of ability...
but because of a lack of participation.

21

CHAPTER 14 — STRUCTURING INVESTING THE RIGHT WAY

Investing does not begin with choosing an asset.

It begins with defining a system.

Most people invest reactively.

They watch the market.

They look for opportunities.

They make decisions based on the moment.

But that approach introduces variability.

And variability destroys consistency.

Because every decision depends on external factors:

Information.

Emotion.

Context.

And when decisions depend on the environment...

the outcome becomes unstable.

That's why effective investing is not built on isolated analysis...

but on structure.

A structure defines three fundamental elements:

When to invest.

How much to invest.

Where to invest.

Without these definitions, any attempt to invest becomes improvised.

And improvisation, over time...

reduces results.

The first element is timing.

Investing should not depend on the moment.

It should happen at defined intervals.

Every cycle.

Every income.

Without exception.

Because consistency removes the need to predict.

You're not trying to find the perfect moment—

you participate in all of them.

This approach reduces decision risk.

And allows time to do its job.

The second element is proportion.

You don't invest what's left.

You invest what is defined.

A portion of your income is already allocated to accumulation.

And within that accumulation...

a portion is directed to investing.

This order is critical.

Because it ensures that investing does not compete with control or stability.

It becomes part of the system—

not a risk to it.

The third element is allocation.

Not all investments serve the same function.

Some provide stability.

Others drive growth.

But the goal is not to find a perfect option.

It's to maintain coherence.

Select a set of instruments aligned with your system...

and remain consistent within them.

Because constant changes reduce the compounding effect.

Investing requires continuity.

This is where most people get it wrong.

They try to optimize each individual decision...

instead of optimizing the entire process.

But the difference is not in getting it right once.

It's in maintaining a structure long enough.

That is the true driver of growth.

This is where the system becomes solid.

You don't invest based on impulse.

You don't invest based on trends.

You invest because it is defined.

Because it is part of the process.

And because every period without investing...

is a period without growth.

This chapter is not about choosing the best investment.

It's about something more important:

Eliminating dependence on timing.

Because when investing is structured...

growth stops depending on isolated decisions...

and starts responding to the system.

And when the system is consistent...

results stop being uncertain.

CHAPTER 15 — SUSTAINING INVESTMENT OVER TIME

Investing does not fail due to a lack of opportunities.

It fails due to a lack of persistence.

Most people are able to start.

They invest once.

Maybe a few more times.

But they don't sustain the process long enough...

for it to produce meaningful results.

This is where the true benefit of the system is lost.

Because growth in investing is not linear.

It does not happen proportionally at the beginning.

It builds progressively...

and only becomes visible after sustained time.

This is where the problem appears.

When results are not immediate, the process is questioned.

The strategy is doubted.

The approach is changed.

Continuity is interrupted.

And by doing so...

the compounding effect resets.

This pattern is common.

Because the mind is wired to respond to the immediate.

It seeks quick validation.

Visible results.

Constant confirmation.

But investing does not operate under that logic.

It operates through sustained accumulation.

The outcome does not depend on a single action...

but on consistent repetition over time.

This is where most people get it wrong.

They confuse the absence of visible results...

with the absence of progress.

But progress is happening.

It's just not visible yet.

This is the moment where the difference is defined.

Not by what you do at the beginning...

but by what you sustain afterward.

Sustaining investing requires eliminating two key factors:

Reaction to the short term.

And the need for constant adjustment.

Because both interrupt the process.

Markets fluctuate.

Conditions change.

Results vary.

But the system should not.

Not because it ignores reality—

but because it is designed to operate within it.

Constantly adjusting based on the moment...

introduces friction.

And friction reduces consistency.

That's why sustaining investing requires a clear decision:

Not to react to every fluctuation.

But to maintain the defined structure.

Invest at the same intervals.

With the same proportions.

Following the same logic.

Without unnecessary interruptions.

This approach removes dependence on timing.

And allows time to do its work.

Because time, in investing, is not an external factor.

It is the core component of the system.

Without time, there is no meaningful accumulation.

Without accumulation, there is no exponential growth.

This is the point where investing stops being an action...

and becomes a process.

A process that does not depend on constant decisions...

but on sustained execution.

And when that execution is maintained...

the outcome stops being uncertain.

Not immediate.

Not visible at first.

But inevitable.

Because the difference is not in how much you invest once.

It's in how long you can sustain it.

And when investing becomes consistent...

growth stops depending on extra effort...

and starts responding to the system.

23

CODE 6 — AUTOMATED INCOME

Up to this point, the system has achieved something fundamental:

Stability.

Control.

Growth.

But there is still a limitation.

Income still largely depends on your direct participation.

You've optimized how money is used.

You've structured how it grows.

But time remains a dominant factor.

And as long as time remains dominant...

the system is not complete.

This is where the next shift occurs.

Not in how money is managed...

but in how it is generated.

Automated income does not eliminate the need to work.

It eliminates total dependence on work.

It allows part of your cash flow to continue...

without constant involvement.

This introduces a new dimension into the system:

Decoupling income from time.

This concept is often misunderstood.

It's associated with instant results, ease, or the complete absence of effort.

But in reality, it works differently.

First, you build.

Then, you maintain.

And over time, you optimize.

Automated income does not appear.

It is designed.

It requires structure.

It requires assets.

It requires a prior process.

But once it exists...

it fundamentally changes how you operate.

Because it introduces something that wasn't there before:

Independent cash flow.

Money that does not depend directly on your daily activity.

This doesn't mean it is completely passive.

It means it is not completely dependent.

And that difference alone...

changes the system.

This is where most people get it wrong.

They pursue automated income too early.

Without control.

Without accumulation.

Without prior investment.

And the result is instability.

Because they attempt to build flow...

without first building a foundation.

This code exists for a specific reason:

To introduce automated income at the right stage of the system.

When control is established.

When accumulation exists.

When investing has begun.

Because at that point...

the process stops being speculative

and becomes structural.

Automated income does not replace the system.

It amplifies it.

It allows growth to no longer depend solely on constant contributions.

And it opens the possibility to scale...

without increasing effort proportionally.

This is the shift.

Not working less—

but no longer depending entirely on work.

Not generating income once—

but building sources that generate it continuously.

And when that happens...

the system reaches a new level.

Money stops being something you only manage or invest...

and starts becoming something that produces.

That is the objective of this code.

Not to create an illusion of ease—

but to establish a process where income can sustain itself...

even when your participation is not constant.

Because when income no longer depends entirely on your time...

the system is no longer bound by linear limits.

And that is where true operational freedom begins.

24

CHAPTER 16 — WHY MOST PEOPLE DON'T GENERATE AUTOMATED INCOME

Most people don't lack opportunities.

They lack structure.

Automated income has become a popular concept—

but also one of the most misunderstood.

It's presented as immediate.

Accessible without a process.

Independent of any prior foundation.

But in reality...

it operates under a completely different logic.

It is not the starting point.

It is the result.

And when it's pursued without a system...

the outcome is inconsistent.

This is the first mistake:

Trying to automate without first building control, accumulation, and investment.

People attempt to generate cash flow without having built a structure.

And the result is predictable:

Unstable income.

Constant dependence.

Lack of continuity.

Because without a foundation, there is no support.

The second mistake is the expectation of ease.

It's assumed that "automated" means effortless.

But automation does not eliminate work.

It shifts it.

You work upfront to build the system.

Then you maintain it with less intervention.

This process is not immediate.

It requires time, structure, and consistency.

But that reality is rarely communicated.

That's why many people quit before building anything that actually works.

The third mistake is dispersion.

People try to create multiple income streams at once.

Different ideas.

Different approaches.

No depth in any of them.

And that dilutes the outcome.

Because automated income is not built through quantity...

it's built through focus.

One well-structured source has more impact than multiple incomplete attempts.

This is where the real pattern appears.

People don't fail because of lack of ability.

They fail because of lack of sequence.

They try to automate without consolidating what comes before.

They try to scale without stabilizing first.

And the system doesn't respond.

Because each level depends on the one before it.

This code does not introduce something new.

It introduces the next logical step.

To transform what has already been built...

into something that can produce without constant intervention.

But for that to happen, the process must be respected.

Control first.

Then accumulation.

Then investment.

And only then—automation.

When that order is followed...

automated income stops being an idea

and becomes a consequence.

That is the point of clarity.

Not pursuing automation as an isolated goal...

but as an extension of the system.

Because when it is built correctly...

income stops depending entirely on direct effort...

and begins to respond to the structure you've created.

And when that happens...

growth is no longer limited by time.

That is the real shift.

And also the reason most people never reach it.

Not because they lack opportunity...

but because they try to arrive

without building first.

25

CHAPTER 17 — HOW TO BUILD AUTOMATED INCOME THE RIGHT WAY

Automated income is not generated.

It is built.

And like anything that is built...

it requires a process.

It does not begin with money.

It begins with an asset.

An asset is any structure capable of producing cash flow on a recurring basis.

It can be financial.

It can be digital.

It can be operational.

But in every case, it serves the same function:

To generate value without requiring constant involvement.

This is where the first principle appears.

You don't build automated income directly.

You build assets that produce it.

This shift in perspective is fundamental.

Because it moves your focus away from the result...

and toward the source.

Most people chase income.

The system builds the origin of that income.

And that difference defines the entire process.

The second principle is the relationship between time and construction.

Automated income does not eliminate work.

It concentrates it.

You invest time upfront to design, structure, and build.

Then that work becomes a foundation...

that can operate with less intervention.

This process is not immediate.

But it is cumulative.

Each asset built becomes part of the system.

And each one expands your capacity to generate cash flow.

The third principle is scalability.

Not all assets have the same growth potential.

Some require ongoing involvement.

Others can expand without increasing effort proportionally.

This code focuses on the latter.

Assets that allow growth...

without complete dependence on your time.

Because that is the objective.

Not to create more work—

but to reduce dependence on it.

This is where construction must be intentional.

It's not about creating any income source.

It's about creating one that can be sustained, repeated, and scaled.

To achieve this, three elements must be defined:

First, the model.

How value is created... and how that value translates into income.

Second, the system.

What processes allow that model to operate consistently.

Third, distribution.

How that income is delivered without requiring constant involvement.

Without these three elements...

income is not automated.

It is dependent.

And dependency maintains the same structural limitation.

This is the most common mistake.

Confusing additional income with automated income.

More sources do not mean more freedom...

if all of them require constant attention.

True automation occurs when the system continues to function...

even as your direct involvement decreases.

That is the standard.

Not how much it generates...

but how much it depends on you.

This is where the focus becomes clear.

Build less... but build better.

Fewer sources.

More structure.

Less dispersion.

More depth.

Because one well-built system...

has greater impact than multiple incomplete attempts.

This chapter is not about simplifying the process.

It's about making it clear.

Because once you understand that the goal is not to generate money...

but to build assets that produce it...

the way you operate changes.

And when the way you operate changes...

results stop depending on direct effort...

and begin to respond to what you've already built.

26

CHAPTER 18 — SCALING AUTOMATED INCOME

Building a source of automated income is progress.

Scaling it is what creates real leverage.

Once an asset generates consistent cash flow, the next step is not to build another one from scratch.

It's to optimize what already works.

Most people make the mistake of spreading themselves too thin.

They build one source.

Then try another.

Then another.

Without fully developing any of them.

And that dilutes the outcome.

Because real growth does not come from the number of sources...

it comes from the ability to expand a functional system.

Scaling means increasing the reach, efficiency, or output of an existing structure.

Not constantly replacing it.

This is where a key distinction appears.

Building requires direct effort.

Scaling requires strategic refinement.

You analyze processes.

You identify points of improvement.

You optimize what is already working.

This approach reduces risk.

Because you are not starting from zero.

You are building on something proven.

The second element of scaling is reinvestment.

The cash flow generated by the system is not fully consumed.

A portion is reinvested.

It is used to expand the capacity of the asset.

More reach.

More volume.

More efficiency.

This process creates a compounding effect.

Each cycle expands the base.

And that base produces more flow.

That flow, when reinvested...

expands the base again.

This is where growth stops being linear.

Because it no longer depends solely on new input.

It depends on the system's ability to expand itself.

This is the point where the system begins to multiply.

But this process requires structural discipline.

Because increased cash flow creates an immediate temptation:

To consume it.

To upgrade lifestyle.

To increase spending.

To relax the structure.
And when that happens...
growth stops.
Reinvestment is what sustains scaling.
Without it, the system may remain...
but it will not expand.
This is where the difference is defined.
Not by how much an asset generates...
but by how much is reinvested to grow.
The third element is simplification.
Scaling does not mean adding complexity.
It means removing friction.
Eliminating unnecessary processes.
Optimizing execution.
Allowing the system to operate more efficiently.
Because a complex system is difficult to sustain.
And what cannot be sustained...
cannot be scaled.
This is the final principle of this code.
Not to constantly build something new—
but to fully develop what already works.
And allow the system to grow on its own foundation.
Because when an asset is scaled correctly...
income stops depending on external expansion...
and starts responding to internal development.
That is the point where the system becomes stronger.
And where growth stops being incremental...
and becomes significant.

27

CODE 7 — WEALTH SCALE

Everything up to this point has built capacity.

This code defines what you do with it.

Because reaching a level where you have control, accumulation, investing, and automated income...

is not the end.

It is the beginning of a new responsibility:

To sustain and multiply.

Wealth is not lost due to lack of income.

It is lost due to lack of structure at higher levels.

As your system grows, so does its complexity.

More cash flow.

More decisions.

More exposure.

And without an evolution in how you operate...

that growth can become unstable.

This is where the real shift happens.

From execution... to direction.

In the previous levels, the focus was on building.

Making direct decisions.

Controlling variables.

Optimizing processes.

But at this level, the focus changes.

It's no longer about doing more.

It's about organizing what already exists.

Scaling wealth involves three fundamental elements:

Consolidation.

Expansion.

Protection.

Consolidation ensures that your foundation is stable.

It's not just about generating...

it's about sustaining.

Clear systems.

Defined structures.

Consistent decisions.

Without consolidation...

growth becomes fragmented.

Expansion, on the other hand, increases reach.

You don't build from scratch.

You replicate what already works.

You optimize it.

You multiply it.

You extend it.

This allows the system to grow...

without increasing effort proportionally.

But expansion without control introduces risk.

That's why the third element is essential:

Protection.

As wealth grows, so does exposure.

Financial risk.

Operational risk.

Decision risk.

Without protection...
the system can regress.
Not because of lack of capability—
but because of lack of foresight.
This is where your approach becomes strategic.
It's no longer just about how much you earn.
It's about how much you keep,
how you allocate it,
and how you protect it over time.
This is the level where wealth stops being a goal...
and becomes a structure.
A structure that does not depend on a single source.
That does not depend on a single decision.
That does not depend on a single person.
That is true scale.
When the system can sustain itself...
expand...
and adapt.
This is where most people stop.
Because this level demands something different:
Long-term thinking.
Not in months—
but in years.
Not in terms of income—
but in terms of assets.
Not in terms of work—
but in terms of systems.
This is the final shift.
From operating to generate...
to operating to sustain and multiply.
And when that shift happens...
money stops being the goal...
and becomes the outcome of the structure.

That is the completion of the system.

Not an ending—

but a state from which everything else is built with clarity.

Because when wealth is organized...

protected...

and expanding...

it no longer depends on constant effort.

It depends on the system.

And when the system is right...

the result is not occasional.

It is inevitable.

28

CHAPTER 19 — CONSOLIDATE BEFORE YOU SCALE

Growth alone is not a sign of stability.

It is a sign of expansion.

And expansion without consolidation...

creates fragility.

This is one of the most common mistakes at advanced levels of the system.

When results begin to appear—more income, more cash flow, more opportunities—

a nearly automatic tendency emerges:

Expand.

New possibilities are identified.

New channels are opened.

More decisions are made.

And on the surface...

everything appears to be moving forward.

But that progress can be deceptive.

Because not all growth is sustainable.

And not all expansion is strategic.

This is where the distinction appears:

Growing... vs. being ready to scale.

Growth increases results.

Scaling multiplies them—without compromising the structure.

And for that to happen...

consolidation is required.

Consolidation is not about stopping growth.

It's about stabilizing it.

It means ensuring that every part of the system operates with clarity, consistency, and autonomy...

before attempting to replicate it.

This process is rarely visible from the outside.

It doesn't create the same excitement as expansion.

It doesn't produce immediate additional results.

But it determines whether the system strengthens...

or becomes vulnerable.

Consolidation requires precision.

Not assuming something works—

but verifying how it works.

Every income stream must be understood:

How it's generated.

What sustains it.

What can affect it.

Every process must be clear.

No unnecessary dependencies.

No ambiguous steps.

No improvised decisions.

And every flow must be controlled:

How much comes in.

How much is retained.

And how it is distributed.

Without this clarity...

the system may function—

but it cannot scale safely.

Because scaling means replication.

And you cannot replicate what you don't fully understand.

This is where most people fail.

They confuse activity with solidity.

They assume that because something produces results...

it is ready to expand.

But producing results is not the same as being consistent.

A system may work under certain conditions—

and fail under others.

It may depend on hidden variables.

On constant decisions.

Or on direct involvement.

And in those cases...

scaling amplifies the problem—

not the result.

That's why consolidation requires something few are willing to do:

Pause expansion... to understand the structure.

Analyze.

Simplify.

Optimize.

Eliminate what is unnecessary.

Strengthen what is essential.

And reduce dependence on unstable variables.

This process does not reduce the system's potential.

It increases it.

Because a consolidated system doesn't just work better—

it becomes replicable.

And replicability...

is the foundation of true scale.

This is where another critical factor appears:

Complexity.

As the system grows, it naturally becomes more complex.

More processes.

More decisions.

More variables.

But complexity is not progress.

In fact, it is one of the greatest risks.

Because a complex system is difficult to understand...

difficult to maintain...

and difficult to scale.

Consolidation aims for the opposite:

Functional simplicity.

Not reducing capacity—

but eliminating friction.

Removing what doesn't add value.

Standardizing what works.

And building a structure that can operate...

without constant intervention.

This is the point where the system begins to mature.

It stops depending on direct effort...

and starts depending on design.

And when that happens...

growth stops being fragile.

It becomes stable.

This is where consolidation fulfills its most important function:

Turning results into structure.

Because as long as results depend on constant action...

they are not scalable.

But when they are embedded in a clear system...
they can be multiplied.
This is the moment where the focus shifts:
From doing more...
to understanding better.
From expanding...
to strengthening.
From reacting...
to designing.
And that shift is what makes the next step—scale—
not a risk... but a logical consequence.
Because when the foundation is solid...
expansion stops being uncertain.
And when the structure is clear...
growth stops depending on additional effort.
That is the purpose of this chapter.
Not to slow progress—
but to prepare it to be sustainable.
Because at higher levels, the goal is not just to grow.
It's to grow without losing stability.
And that only happens when what already exists...
is fully consolidated.

29

CHAPTER 20 — MULTIPLY WHAT ALREADY WORKS

Early growth requires creation.

Scaling requires selection.

When a system begins to generate results, the challenge is no longer to produce more.

It is to decide where to focus.

This is one of the most critical points in the entire process.

Because at this level...

opportunities multiply.

New ideas.

New offers.

New directions.

And each one appears valid.

But not all are strategic.

This is where most people go off track.

They confuse expansion with dispersion.

They begin building multiple paths at once.

They divide their attention.

They fragment their resources.

And the result is predictable:

They lose depth.

Because what is constantly divided...

never fully develops.

This is where the core principle of this chapter emerges:

Scaling is not about doing more.

It's about growing what already works.

This shift in perspective is decisive.

Because it eliminates the need to start from zero...

and allows you to leverage what has already been proven.

A system that already produces results has something no new idea has:

Evidence.

It works under real conditions.

It has demonstrated consistency.

It has structure.

Multiplying it is not speculation.

It is strategy.

But this requires something specific:

The discipline to eliminate what is unnecessary.

Not everything that can be done...

should be done.

And at higher levels, this decision becomes more important than any action.

Because every new direction comes with a cost:

More time.

More energy.

More complexity.

And poorly managed complexity...

reduces efficiency.

That's why scaling requires precision.

Identifying which part of the system creates the greatest impact...

and concentrating resources there.

Expanding its reach.

Optimizing its operation.

Increasing its capacity.

Without altering its core.

This is where growth becomes intelligent.

It is not based on quantity.

It is based on focus.

A well-developed system can be multiplied in multiple ways:

More clients.

Greater distribution.

Higher internal efficiency.

But all of these come from the same source:

A solid foundation.

This is the mistake many people make.

They try to diversify before they master.

They expand before they consolidate.

They multiply before they fully understand.

And by doing so...

they dilute what already works.

This is where strategic discipline comes in.

Not reacting to every opportunity—

but filtering every decision through a clear question:

Does this strengthen what already works...

or does it dilute it?

If it strengthens, it's considered.

If it dilutes, it's eliminated.

This filter changes everything.

Because it allows the system to grow in depth...

before it grows in breadth.

And that depth...
is what makes real scale possible.
This is where growth stops depending on new ideas...
and starts depending on continuous development.
This is the point where the system matures.
Where execution stops being reactive...
and becomes deliberate.
And where every action is driven by strategy—
not by momentary opportunity.
That is the purpose of this chapter.
Not to generate more...
but to multiply better.
Because when what already works is fully developed...
growth stops being uncertain.
And becomes a direct consequence of focus.

30

CHAPTER 21 — PROTECTING AND SUSTAINING WEALTH

Building wealth is a process.

Sustaining it is a discipline.

As the system grows, so do its risks.

Not only financial—

but operational...

and often invisible.

This is where many systems fail.

Not because of lack of capability...

but because of lack of foresight.

They focus on generating.

On growing.

On expanding.

But not on protecting.

And what is not protected...

is eventually lost.

This is where the final evolution of the system takes place.

Not in how to produce more...

but in how to sustain what already exists.

Because at higher levels, the objective changes.

It is no longer just about growth.

It's about maintaining, preserving, and ensuring continuity.

This requires something specific:

Reducing vulnerability.

Not depending on a single source.

Not centralizing critical decisions.

Not operating without safeguards.

At this level, diversification is no longer optional.

It becomes essential.

But not as random expansion—

as strategic distribution.

Different income streams.

Different structures.

Different levels of exposure.

This ensures that the system does not depend on a single variable.

And when a system is not dependent on one factor...

it becomes resilient.

The second element is organization.

As wealth grows, informality becomes a risk.

Unstructured decisions.

Unclear processes.

Undefined responsibilities.

All of this creates friction.

And at higher levels...

friction becomes expensive.

That's why organization becomes critical.

Define structures.

Separate functions.

Maintain clear control.

Because an organized system...
is a sustainable system.
The third element is discipline.
Not relaxing the system when results are strong.
This is one of the most common mistakes.
When everything is working...
people lower their guard.
Rules are loosened.
Impulsive decisions are made.
The system is assumed to be unbreakable.
But it isn't.
And it is precisely at that moment...
when structure matters most.
Because wealth is not lost at the beginning.
It is lost in the relaxation.
This is the final level of operation.
Not just building.
Not just scaling.
But sustaining.
Sustaining over time.
Sustaining across conditions.
Sustaining beyond direct involvement.
This is where the system stops being a set of actions...
and becomes a structure that endures.
It does not depend on a moment.
It does not depend on a single decision.
It depends on how it is built.
And when it is built correctly...
it can be sustained.
That is the ultimate objective.
Not just to create wealth—
but to build a system capable of preserving it,
protecting it,

and sustaining it over time.

Because in the end...

the difference is not in how much you earn.

It's in how much you keep...

and for how long.

PART III

PART 3 — ACTIVATION

Understanding a system does not create results.

Applying it does.

Up to this point, you have moved through every level of the process:

You've understood the structural mistake.

You've built control.

You've eliminated friction.

You've accumulated.

You've invested.

You've created flow.

And you've seen how to scale it.

But none of that has value...

unless it becomes execution.

This is where most people stop.

Not because they lack ability—

but because they fail to transition.

They consume information.

They understand concepts.

They recognize patterns.

But they do not act with structure.

And without structure...

action becomes inconsistent.

They try.

They stop.

They start again.

And the system never becomes solid.

That is why this section exists.

Not to explain more—

but to activate.

Not to add more content—

but to define execution.

From this point forward, the focus changes completely.

From understanding...

to doing.

From analyzing...

to deciding.

From planning...

to operating.

No new ideas are introduced here.

What comes next is the organization of everything you've already learned into a clear process.

A plan.

Not generic.

Not abstract.

But actionable.

Step by step.

Without ambiguity.

Without dependence on motivation.

Because motivation does not sustain results.

Structure does.

This is the moment where the final difference is defined.

Not by what you know—

but by what you do with it.

You can understand this entire system...

and remain exactly where you are.

Or you can execute with precision...

and completely change your trajectory.

The difference is not in the content.

It is in the decision.

And that decision happens here.

Not tomorrow.

Not when conditions are perfect.

Now.

Because the system does not need more information.

It needs implementation.

And from this point forward...

that is exactly what you are going to do.

31

YOUR WEALTH SYSTEM PLAN — STEP BY STEP

A system only has value when it is executed.

Everything you've read up to this point can be reduced to a clear sequence.

You do not need more information.

You need order.

This is the plan.

Not theoretical.

Not optional.

It is how the system becomes results.

Step 1 — Establish Total Control

Before you move forward, you must know exactly what is happening with your money.

How much comes in.

How much is retained.

And where it is going.

Without clarity...

there can be no correct decision.

Over the next few days, track everything.

Don't adjust anything yet.

Don't try to optimize.

Just observe.

Because you cannot change...

what you do not understand.

Step 2 — Define Your Financial Structure

Once you have visibility, you establish rules.

What percentage goes to expenses.

What percentage is retained.

What percentage is prepared for growth.

This structure is not negotiable.

It is applied to every income.

Without exception.

Because what is constantly negotiated...

is never sustained.

Step 3 — Eliminate Friction (Debt)

If you have debt, this is the next focus.

Do not disperse your effort.

Do not improvise.

Set a clear priority.

Attack one debt at a time.

With consistency.

Until it is gone.

Every debt that disappears...

releases capacity.

And that capacity is what you need to move forward.

Step 4 — Activate Accumulation

Once the system is under control, you begin to build your foundation.

You do not save what is left over.

You accumulate first.

A fixed percentage.

From every income.

Without interruption.

This is not optional.

It is the foundation of everything that follows.

Step 5 — Begin Investing

Once accumulation exists, money must begin to produce.

Do not wait for the perfect moment.

Do not try to get it exactly right.

Participate.

Consistently.

At defined intervals.

Because growth does not depend on one decision...

it depends on repetition.

Step 6 — Build a Source of Automated Income

With foundation, control, and investing in place, now you build.

You do not chase money.

You build an asset.

Something that can generate flow on a continuous basis.

Not multiple attempts.

One well-structured source.

And you develop it until it works.

Step 7 — Scale What Works

When something produces results, you do not change direction.

You expand it.

More reach.

More efficiency.

More capacity.

Do not disperse.

Go deeper.

Because real growth comes from what is fully developed.

Step 8 — Protect and Sustain

As the system grows, you must maintain it.
Do not relax the rules.
Do not improvise decisions.
Diversify.
Organize.
Protect.
Because building wealth is difficult.
But losing it is fast.
This is the complete plan.
You do not need to do it perfectly.
You need to do it consistently.
Not everything at once.
Step by step.
But without stopping.
Because the system does not work through intensity.
It works through continuity.
This is where everything is decided.
Not by what you understood...
but by what you are willing to execute.
This plan does not change.
It does not depend on trends.
It does not depend on external conditions.
It depends on you.
And if you execute it as it was designed...
the outcome is not uncertain.
It is inevitable.

32

FROM READER TO EXECUTOR

Reading does not change results.

Execution does.

This is the point where everything that came before is defined.

Not by the quality of the content.

Not by what you understood.

But by what you are willing to do from this moment forward.

Most people make it this far.

They read.

They understand.

They relate to it.

And then...

nothing changes.

Not because the system doesn't work—

but because they never implement it.

That is the pattern.

Information is consumed as if it were progress.

But progress does not happen in reading.

It happens in execution.

This is the moment where that cycle is broken.

Because you do not need more clarity.

You already know what to do.

You already know the order.

You already know why it works.

The only thing left is a decision:

Stay where you are...

or operate differently.

There is no real middle ground.

Because any partial change without structure...

eventually leads back to the same place.

This is where the real difference becomes visible.

Not between those who know more—

but between those who execute.

Execution does not require perfection.

It requires a start.

It requires taking the first step without waiting for ideal conditions.

Because those conditions do not exist.

There will always be uncertainty.

There will always be variables.

There will always be reasons to wait.

But waiting does not build.

Execution does.

This system does not depend on motivation.

It depends on repetition.

It does not depend on intense beginnings.

It depends on consistency.

That is why real change does not happen in a single moment.

It happens through the accumulation of correct decisions.

One after another.

Without unnecessary interruption.

This is the point where you become an operator.

Where you stop reacting...

and start directing.

Where money stops being something that comes and goes...

and becomes something that is organized, grown, and sustained.

But that does not happen automatically.

It happens when you decide to apply what you already understand.

You do not need more theory.

You do not need more validation.

You need to begin.

Today.

Not with everything.

But with something.

The first step.

Then the next.

And after that—maintain it.

Because that is what builds the outcome.

Not one isolated action—

but a sustained sequence.

This book will not change your life.

What you do after reading it will.

And that "after" begins now.

Not when you have more time.

Not when everything feels clear.

Now.

Because the system is already defined.

And the only thing left...
is for you to put it into motion.

33

THE POINT OF NO RETURN

There comes a moment when you can no longer go back.

Not because something external changes—

but because you now understand too much.

That moment is not visible.

It doesn't happen when you finish a chapter.

It doesn't happen when you grasp a concept.

It happens when you see the system as a whole...

and recognize, with absolute clarity, that staying the same is a choice.

From this point forward, you can no longer say you didn't know.

You can no longer justify your results with a lack of information.

Because now you understand:

How money is lost.

How it is organized.

How it is built.
And how it is multiplied.
And once that clarity exists...
ignorance is no longer an excuse.
This is where a different kind of discomfort appears.
It's not doubt.
It's not confusion.
It's awareness.
You know you could do better.
You know you could operate differently.
And you know that not doing it...
is also a decision.
This is the point of no return.
Because from here, there are only two paths.
The first is familiar.
Continue as you always have.
Make small adjustments.
Try occasionally.
Return to the same patterns.
Nothing truly changes.
It is simply maintained.
The second path is different.
Not more complex.
Not more difficult.
But more conscious.
It requires applying what you already understand.
Without perfection.
Without drama.
But without going backward.
This is where most people fail.
Not in their ability—
but in their decision.

Because change does not require knowing more.

It requires stopping the negotiation with yourself.

Stopping the justification of what you already know doesn't work.

And starting to execute—

even when it's not comfortable.

This moment is not emotional.

It is logical.

If you understand the system...

and do not apply it...

the result is not uncertainty.

It is continuity.

More of the same.

That is the real cost.

Not the mistake—

but the repetition.

This chapter does not exist to motivate you.

It exists to make one thing clear:

From this point forward, everything depends on you.

Not on the environment.

Not on the market.

Not on luck.

On how you choose to operate.

Because the system is already defined.

And when a system is defined...

the outcome is not a possibility.

It is a consequence.

The only variable left...

is whether you execute.

This is the point of no return.

Not because something changes outside—

but because now you know.

And once you know...
staying the same is no longer neutral.
It becomes a choice.
And now...
that choice is yours.

THE SYSTEM AND TIME

Money doesn't change people.
It reveals them.
It amplifies what already exists.
It exposes decisions.
And it reflects how a person has lived up to that point.
That's why this book was never truly about money.
It was about structure.
How you decide.
How you organize.
And how you build over time.
Because money, at its core...
is a consequence.
Not of a single moment—
but of a sustained system.
That system is not formed through big decisions.
It is formed through repetition.
In what you do every time you receive income.
In what you choose to keep.

In what you decide to build.

Day after day.

Cycle after cycle.

Even when it's not visible at first.

This is where time becomes the most important factor.

Not as something that passes—

but as something that accumulates.

Time amplifies whatever is already structured.

If the system is weak, time exposes it.

If the system is strong, time multiplies it.

That is the difference.

Not between those who are lucky and those who aren't—

but between those who operate with intention...

and those who operate without structure.

Throughout this book, the focus has been clear:

Eliminate what slows you down.

Build what sustains you.

Develop what grows.

But none of that happens in a single moment.

It happens through continuity.

Through decisions that, on their own, seem small...

but when accumulated, change everything.

This is the point most people fail to see.

Because they look for visible change immediately.

But reality works differently.

Visible results are the consequence...

of invisible processes sustained over time.

This system does not promise speed.

It promises direction.

It does not eliminate effort.

It organizes it.

And by doing so, it allows time to stop being a limitation...

and become an advantage.

That is the real value.

Not how much money you can generate in a moment—

but how strong the system is that sustains it.

Because when the system is right...

growth does not depend on perfect conditions.

It depends on continuity.

And continuity, over time...

becomes decisive.

This is where everything simplifies.

You don't need to do more.

You need to do what is right... consistently.

You don't need to get it right once.

You need to sustain a process.

Because in the end...

the difference is not one extraordinary decision.

It is the repetition of correct decisions

for long enough.

That is the system.

And now you understand it.

The only thing left...

is to live it.

MEET THE AUTHOR: THE FOUNDER OF INSPIRED LEGACY PRESS

Edgar Hernández is an author, speaker, and architect of human transformation. He is the founder of **Inspired Legacy Press**, an independent publishing imprint through which he leads a global movement dedicated to the mastery and evolution of human potential.

His work integrates **philosophy, science, and behavioral psychology** with emotional intelligence, neuro-biohacking, performance biology, longevity science, high-level habits, and systematic physical development to cultivate **mental clarity, inner strength, and unbreakable discipline.**

He is the creator of the **Inspired Legacy Framework**, a system of human transformation built upon four dimensions: **identity, body, wealth, and spirit.**

This framework is designed for individuals who choose to forge character, master their vital energy, expand their awareness, and build a life defined by real results rather than temporary motivation.

Through his books and teachings, he maintains a central conviction:

Those who master their mind, their emotions, and their habits... master their destiny.

This book forms part of an **Editorial System** conceived for the integral transformation of the individual.

A system built upon principles, structure, and long-term vision, where each work fulfills a precise role within a greater whole: cultivating **mental clarity, self-discipline, inner strength, and a conscious identity** capable of sustaining real results across the four dimensions of human development—**identity, body, wealth, and spirit.**

The purpose of the **Inspired Editorial System** is to refine judgment, elevate thinking, and forge character.

Each book is a pillar.

Each concept is a tool for real life.

This system is intended for those who understand that **personal growth is not a trend, but a deliberate and structured practice**—that freedom is built through knowledge, decision, and coherence—and that every true legacy begins in **the architecture of the mind.**

This is not self-help.

This is human architecture.

Master your identity.

Strengthen your body.

Multiply your wealth.

Expand your spirit.

Build power.

Build freedom.

Build legacy.

Welcome to the Inspired Universe.

instagram.com/edgarhernandezofficial

facebook.com/EdgarHernandezOfficial

youtube.com/@EdgarHernandezOfficial

Made in United States
Orlando, FL
04 November 2026

90203410R00088